LAMB

Also by Michael Kenyon

FICTION

Kleinberg
Pinocchio's Wife
Durable Tumblers
The Biggest Animals
The Beautiful Children
A Year at River Mountain
Parallel Rivers

POETRY

Rack of Lamb
The Sutler
The Last House
Astatine

CHAPBOOKS

Winter Wedding
Twig
Broad Street Blues
Ottawa

LAMB

Michael Kenyon

PEDLAR PRESS
ST. JOHN'S

COVER ART   Lorraine Thomson, detail, *Whitemud*
DESIGN   Mark Byk
TYPEFACES   Dair & Stempel Garamond
Printed in Canada at Coach House Printing, Toronto ON

LIBRARY AND ARCHIVES CANADA CATALOGUING IN PUBLICATION
Kenyon, Michael, 1953-, author
      Lamb / Michael Kenyon.

POEMS.
Edited by Stan Dragland.
ISBN 978-1-897141-91-5 (SOFTCOVER)

      I. Dragland, Stan, 1942-, editor II. Title.

PS8571.E67L35 2018   C811'.54   C2018-903892-6

First Edition

ACKNOWLEDGEMENTS
The publisher wishes to thank the Canada Council for the Arts and the NL Publishers Assistance Program for their generous support of our publishing program.

Canada Council   Conseil des arts
for the Arts   du Canada

Newfoundland
Labrador

To those I've loved on Pender Island

Contents

Between the parietal bones of the skull
Swings the sagittal door, as the lobe swings
Behind the palate. Through that one goes out…
                              —*The Taittiriya Upanishad*

What were we, then,
Before the being of ourselves began?
                              —Laura Riding

Ottawa

Arc
The Hill
Alexandra Bridge
The Barley Mow

Arc
Time present and time past

I

Dropped my earbud in hot coffee calling
Lorraine on the smartphone. *Landed.* We talked
about teeth, our failing teeth, the nest egg
gone to canals, crowns, extractions, amen.

I love you, sipped the coffee, and she said:
This is not a bad life, right? and I said,
Thanks to non-locality, and uncapped
my fountain pen and scribbled: *Ottawa.*

The Zen-pen's deformed white-gold nib, dated
April, 1974, Japan,
wrote through Mumbai, jotted its blue way
via eBay to Vancouver and now

has soared Rockies, prairies and Great Lakes to
Ottawa. Waiting for the bath to fill,
I doodle Vedantic calculations:
Japan to India, India to

vegetable biryani, aloo
paratha, papadam, mutter paneer.

Quick, says the bird, catch the worm while you can.
Do you remember? Where does this come from?

Two robins always roost in the cedar
by the alder gate and when we come home
at dusk they fly off, don't return, and we
apologize, sorry for all we have

mist-netted: thrushes, orioles, catbirds,
tanagers, vireos, buntings, warblers,
restless, restless, quick to fly our naming,
for we have not earned the right to trouble

even those we know well. Listen, they call
to us from the same places day after
day: fence, wire, roof, crane, tower, pole, scaffold,
rail, spire, gutter, overpass, bridge, highrise.

All meaning is less than meaning. Where does
this come from? From the same place as water.
Fire is less than wet. Where does this come from?
Same place. The man disappeared without
a trace. Who was this man? A trace. He will
be you when your last question has faded.

In early morning I walked Rue Metcalfe
from the Arc Hotel, climbed Parliament Hill
for bearings, found a sea-green pagoda
and a dented iron bell. Travel haunts
our cells where we are, not where we were.
Life's not a still-life cabaret, old chum,

though bronze men pose with women at their feet
around a whole gang of green copper roofs,
and I wrote a novel about a man
who sets out to find what he's forgotten,
and the novel won a prize and I'm here
to collect a ring and recognition.

River trees flame red up in Gatineau.
Ottawa is being repaved with gold.
A range of bridges upriver, bridges
downstream. Warm morning sun on my jacket.
Tongue seeks to soothe the flap of skin come loose
from my back molar. Have I enough time?

III

This bell struck midnight, February third,
Nineteen-sixteen, rang through white flames, then crashed
Through the old stone bell tower. Remember?

Third day of antibiotic healing,
third week of nursing a sore groin pull,
my system's uproarious. Without sleep
I lie on the hotel bed and stare out
at the grey-textured concrete wall that beeps
its mass. It is what is left of silence,
along with white noise from the corridor,
traffic streams past the front of the hotel.
Once tiny yellow leaves drift in the gap
between my window and the blank grey wall.

Rage in Europe, a cigar in the trash.
Centre Block women run for fur coats, cold
Wind chases smoke from the ice-cased ruins.

Snowflakes once. No one can see in or out.
This could be any room in the world,
but it is mine and I am here, now.
Once a leather work-glove spinning, waving.
Down in the lobby no doubt other guests
are checking in, toasting with white wine, nothing
to do with time. Such confounded strange lives
cross the raw street all day, women and men
wander the flagged and fenced construction zone,
quick views of the National Arts Centre.

Centre Block burned all night. The way, the way
The burning tower held the ringing bell
Until it fell, until the tower fell.

How caption such a gesture to stillness?
Nothing on TV, minibar a bust,
window a blue screen, no history here.
Yet the lakes and red and yellow copses
we flew over yesterday were lovely
in evening light, registered along
with the Nepalese Canadian girl,
and my novel on the night stand's open
to Sapporo and Star, father and son,
still hunting, still losing each other.

IV

This swift horizon line almost prairie,
the opposing bank its own blaze of fall.

A jointed silver finger dangles from
a crane by the National Gallery.

How many times will the terrified men
stand on guard? How many times will they rise?

Across the Ottawa River, ruins
of E.B. Eddy's Digester Tower.

We rise to name our country. Our country.
Our commonwealth is our... personal time.

V

Personal time accrues invisibly
in the eyes, but on the edges sea foam,
snow or ashes blur all the partitions,
fences, to soft round shapes and arctic blue,
unexplored, as we abandon words and
simply look, until the flint of our time
strikes the stone of all time and sparks ignite
the small dry fuel each of us allows,
carefully isolates, from the storehouse
of our hurried and glorious passage.

Another larger impersonal beast
has hunted the banks of this wide river.
Soon you'll see its stealth commemorated
on plaques, mud its paw disturbed one fine spring
in filibuster, cannonade, or wild
protest among cop cars, bodyguards, riled
supreme court judges, soldiers and statues.
Hill librarians and clerks continue
to map the monster's savage kills along
the boundaries between owned and free land.

Black Felt Hat

I can't afford to buy a book because
I am an unsuccessful scribe. Now there's
two lines of iambic pentameter.

The Indian boy wanted to play me
a song. *Sponsor me and I'll sing you up*,
he called. *Where did you get that native hat?*
I touched the brim and he laughed. Who were we
kidding: we only recognized pale / dark
versions of ourselves fooling in the wind,
late for a lecture, too nervous to stop.

The Hill

In my beginning is my end

I

The sea is young,
Not planned. (*Try again*
With rhythm and rhyme.
Don't be ashamed.
Same words, same song.)
But the sea falters
For want of voices.
  The river begun
Yesterday in the north
Between winter and spring
Passed us moments ago:
Hub and spokes,
Old aqueduct
Furred with frost,
Pail and handle. (*Retreat*
To your hearths, lock
Eyes on the screen,
You can't mend the rift
Between summer and fall.)
  Logos :o) Eros :o(
To hell with the old
Estuary choir, its
Circle-Stone Song.

Two crows and three soldiers scream, transmute,
bronze feathers and rifles alert, alive.
All this talk of reconciliation,
confederation, both sides of the bridge.

Then, holding the line, GPS aloft,
looking for my hotel, needing to shit,
I lose myself in the Glebe, in Bytown,
among panhandlers and students, pumping

a long mossy echo of *Four Quartets.*
Old Sapporo has trekked as far as this
valley, to this red corner of winter.
My forgotten world-creating hero

fording the river, skirting monuments,
a shadow at this winter festival,
is one of my kind, one of many
indirect routes to self-discovery.

Just a quick shit at the National Arts
before Ken Dryden, York Centre Dryden,
ex-Habs goalie, Leafs president, launches
Becoming Canada, another route,

another trade wind. He says politics
is an obstacle to discussions of
what Canada is, and Canada is
a symptom set of the lack of something

on the table. What Canada will be
is under the table, a begging dog,
a slinking cat, a fat child, a hairball,
nuts and bolts of a brand new invention.

At the end of assembly comes the use
of what has been assembled: the swamp gate.
Multiculturalism gives way to
multiculture and I tongue my sore gum.

To get energized again, Dryden says,
you have to leave the Hill. It's exhausting…
parliament's a de-energizing place,
public debate's an exchange of punchlines.

What we need are tales, the lives and stories
behind the punchlines.
                      The oldest fish,
the promise it made when we let it go,
wounded. Must the fish stay wounded to heal?

Must the alder gate stay closed, the robins
undisturbed, animals in the forest?
People in the city. Kids in the park.
Poet in his caravan in the swamp.

On the street again we are turned around
but the city begins to remember
itself and soon we find our way home to
the Arc, to grey wall, bar, bed and TV.
Sapporo quietly in my pocket
in the closet. I've promised to read him,
but am uncertain about reading Star,
he's allergic to light, couldn't care less.
           Yes, Sapporo, yes.
           A novel fakes truth,
takes leave from life's complications. Lobbies
empty and fill. Introductions cannot
go on. The novel builds counting house,
palace, withdrawing room, sanctuary,
crypt, battlement, moat, airport, bell tower,
then assembles highways, farms and cities,
           a father and son.
           Then father and son
wander down the lane beside the river
long ago. They wind things up, wind up here:
the Arc Hotel hospitality suite.

III

In time we get to the fragments, the black
pieces fallen out of the sun, and try
(what am I doing? where does this come from?)
to guess the whole or fill in the spaces
with whatever's to hand: a furry moth,
a still frog, a wad of compressed brown leaves,
the great horned owl from the bare maple branch
outside the outhouse, or transcendental
childhood: the boy swimming at Morfa Nefyn,
the young man at The Undersea Gardens.

    The dark dance
    Invented for harlequin
    Phosphorescence for starlight
    Pale face for deep water
    Sea's softness for frost
    Volcanic for islands
    The grain for food
    Tides for the moon
    Earth for sea
    Beginnings for déjà vu
    What we make
    For what we are
    What we are
    Four seasons
    What we do forever
    Tree by falling tree
    Cliff by falling cliff

IV

The wounded sturgeon
lived at The Gardens
where I swam after a failed career
in roofing. From a winter of raw knees
and blistered thumbs I put on a wetsuit,
strapped on lead and tank and regulator,
swam beside the big battered ancient fish,
her eyes broadcasting unforgivable
stories from the bottom of the river.
                          She,
bottom-fed, solitary, scaleless,
fine grey leather hard and smooth to the touch,
her eyes living nothing, nothing to live.
Tattered barbels swaying with the current
of her slow going and slower turns, and
                          me
matching her turns all the way around
the riveted space, thinking I was free.

I witnessed but did not yet recognize
my first guide to the other world; older
than time, she redefined silver, ghosting
the line of shaggy green electric lamps,
her nose blunted and bloody from banging
the steel sides of her tank.
                          Cephalopods
came to die. Sea feather, anemone,
ratfish, dogfish, skate, crab, lasted a month,
but her antique brain, tethered to sun,
                          felt
its way into centuries of darkness.
My first guide to the other world, wounded
of course, unscientific, burned steady.

V

Underwater Garden diver
Jumpsuited girl selling starfish
Engineer in the pump house

Fresh sea labyrinth
Iron heart of bolted pipes
Coloured valves and dials

Hospitality Suite

Not my first or last guide to something lost.
Where does this come from, this trace of carbon?

Isinglass, mercury, gold, all worthless,
won't even burn, but will carry meaning.

Might naming the guides and their currency
open a new path in the synapses?

(These bright clouds churning, backdrop to islands,
channels seagulls navigate dusk and dawn.)

Every writer is a guide to something
if not lost then stolen, forgotten, spurned.

The food is bite-sized, cheesecake before beef;
plenty of beer, plenty of red and white.

The writers are bite-sized, beef before cheesecake;
plenty of bluff, plenty of green and blue.

(These dark clouds churning, backdrop to cities,
to channels gulls navigate, wind and storm.)

Empty by midnight, except for the hosts
arguing about tradition and cheats.

> Wood energy
> In this room needs to release,
> Needs to flow, but where?

> Outside the hotel
> Wind blows cold, red stars
> Spark from cigarettes.

> My ploughed head's full
> Of names of writers, books; path
> Too hard for old bones

Leads the risen boy
To a dark field, and a
Pocketful of seeds

Sows wild the jungle
To a carved oak Wurlitzer
Garlanded in the clearcut.

Every spring I build
A fire from winter deadfall
Storms snap from alder.

Who would *I* invite
Around a deadfall fire
In the last winter?

Alexandra Bridge
I do not know much about gods

I

Along Rue Metcalfe past Sparks Street around Parliament
Centre Block over the Hill, cut down to the canal path, cross a
closed lock and up the next hill to the National Gallery, silver
finger, absent crane.

Down to the cantilevered bridge and over the river just like that
is all there is to language, story and poetry, all one-step, two-
step, one province then the next, just like that, and fight the
impulse to count or name or break the line. *Swing your partner,
promenade home.*

> Too poor to dance
> Too poor to love
> Too poor to laugh
> Too poor to aim high
> Too poor to sleep
> Too poor to travel far

And stop at the white basilica, Notre Dame, the white
cathedral, for almost a vision. But antibiotics are anti-trance.
The resulting struggle gives me bloodwaves and ocular flares as
I sit in a pew rocked by the rhythm of the central nave,
transfixed by sanctuary and main altar, and can't keep still.
Accompanied by Adam and Mary and a battalion of saints,
I cross the gravel street.

> Bosch, *The Temptation of St. Anthony* (1499)
> Rubens, *The Entombment* (1612)
> Turner, *Shoeburyness Fishermen Hailing
>   a Whitstable Hoy* (1809)
> Courbet, *The Cliffs at Étretat* (1866)
> Vincento, *Iris* (1889)
> Monet, *A Stormy Sea* (1896)
> Braque, *The Glass of Absinthe* (1910)
> Matisse, *Nude on a Yellow Sofa* (1926)

And now, Mother and Father, let's begin
to troubleshoot our lives, see what went wrong.
One went left, one went right: disturbance,
famine and war, organized voyages.

> Port and starboard
> Plank and pitch
> Rib and strut
> Deck and rigging
> Tooth and nail
> Tongue and groove
> Brick and wood
> Lath and plaster
> Frame and pole
> Mortise and tenon
> Irish and Irish
> Odawa Algonquin
> American and French
> Scottish and Cornish
> Fox and hounds
> Bric-a-brac
> Scheißerei
> Hunt and kill
> Kiss and tell
> Heaven and earth
> Bride and groom
> Barn and stable

And soon I'll learn my sister is my half-
sister, that Mum went left when Dad went right,
my middle path always veering deep north
across the field to the stile to the truth.

III

Cold and colder with wind. Rain in the night
has brought these pearl clouds. What to do
after prayer in Notre Dame but wonder
at the board-and-canvas dreams that transcend
life, the fifteenth-century workshops that
perfected translucent tears, fine brocades,
what to make of cut-and-spliced religious
myth, feast tables where men and women wait
for dead animals, and angels decry
biblical dysfunction while storms rage stern
figures off their ground, painters forget their
purpose and the main character smuggles
himself and his nude girl out of the frame.

Uncorrupt aquarium, museum,
all our gardens now are behind glass,
bounded by glass, inside time, inside place,
and we tap tap tap the glass, the garden
flexes, winks, does a curtsy, and we know
what we know is nothing like anything
(sojourns on the other side of the glass),
is all about performance, all an act
for an audience of similar selves,
no surprise to be wired up to gauges
for the final leap from the last cliff, though
we still don't know how deep the water is.

IV

Limping through Ottawa with a torn
groin and wounded gum to accept a ring.

Where do we belong now the harvest's in?
Death is in all winter things. The river

blackly purple tonight, glassy, smooth,
stark tautology of dark and light.

Bridges and roads busy with traffic,
glossy cars heading all the way home, or

there must be other less visible streams
easy to find, say frog, say worm, say bee.

Say sleep, say laughter, say dance, say love, say
Odawa, a seed sleeping in the earth.

The bridge from Ottawa to Gatineau
redecked by young Frenchmen hung chatting

in the undercrofts with arc welders, tape
and pencil, Skilsaw, hand trolleys of planks

half new, half old—their words still midriver,
tugged downstream but attentive to the work.

What was that falling dream? A boy leaping
from a tower into unknown water.

How many times does the terrified boy leap?
How many times die? How many survive?

V

A day at the Gallery took me in-
to the frame, onto faintly pink granite
blocks, café with glass ceiling high above,
the river below, parliament atop
its hill. This view built for Colonel By's stone
cottage and English gardens, a thousand
men killed heaving and laying canal stones.

Two hundred years, four hundred, eight hundred.
New rooms and rooms of paintings, too many
to comprehend. Church work, patron work, and
Jackson Pollock twitching like a mad man,
as Holden Caulfield would say, rectangles
of canvas, rectangles of glass, with beads
and wire and whatever's to hand.
                                        We end

and begin
                hoping for a girl half-fish
to follow the current where the river
scoops sand and pebbles from the old seabed,
so something we can't catch in ourselves will
catch in her, catch and begin to rise. Channel,
route, schedule, career, destiny, pact.
Small bubbles escape from long-held breath.

A Mermaid on Sparks Street

will tell the nation's fortune.
Let's hope for a son half-bird
to descry the old patterns
of irrigation, ditch work
we're too old and stuck to see
we've pasted onto cities.

Let's walk to the edge of town,
those of us with time to spare,
and look out at the dark ground,
taste the mix of smoke and air,
let's trade our nation's decline
for once-wild villages.

We won't be happy until
we've captioned this spindrift
nation, this nation's capital,
told the earth it's ours to sift,
our old fingers dry and slow,
to see what makes sense to grow.

The Barley Mow

Midwinter spring is its own season

I

Villagers, why do we hold to this place? Winter misbehaving, our children lost, breaking through the river ice. We should leave this gathering, stocktaking, provisional way station next spring. Have we not, in our mind's eye, seen another valley, sunny and fragrant, with perfect confluence of water, hill and sky?

You were there as a child. My father was there when he was a child. And you, you've been there in dreams. Have we missed the sign that told us to return? Did you forget, when you married, to set the alarm? Did I neglect to register the days of my stay at the front desk? Does my sister know who she is? Do we know who we are? Have I lost my hat already?

We hold to this seeded field and find ourselves tilling at the cold crack of dawn and mowing the grain at the end of a summer day. We hold to this melting field and yearn for the other valley, afraid to name where we are and where we have been in case the difference between here and there is the difference between never and always.

> The mother's independence
> Gainsays the boy's
> And the man sleeps on the floor
> By his lover's crowded bed

                    We begin
here in Ottawa, me and Sapporo
and Star, opposite Virgin and Christ
on the sanctuary wall, to witness
everything rising to where it can be
seen, teeth, buds, spoons, pipes, cups, swords, hearts. I kneel
in a pew in Notre Dame Cathedral,
quietest room in the city, and
listen to the tinkling busyness of
a stout woman arranging candle jars,
and watch light throb and flow and throb with the
bashing of my pulse behind closed lids.
                    Why
must I compare myself with what I have
created? Must *The Beautiful Children*
judge me? Why am I here at all? *Am* I
here at all?
                    Singsong of immigration.
Birds fly pell-mell from the understory
to perch on branches and address the boy.
The green field sways, the grain has gone to seed.
Listen to them return, the flocks and flocks,
my third tier of guides, flitty songbirds;
then hawks plummet. I'm scared to take a breath
without first checking right and left, Father
and Mum, my dog, my sister, my wife.
And why are they here now I'm nearly old?
To see have I added anything new?

        From this height a man
        Gauges the difference
        Between Ottawa and London
        Finds river trees flame-red

        And a tall yellow crane
        Dangling a silver finger
        The streets not paved with gold
        But with October sunshine

              Why
compare myself with others? With every
writer who ever lived, every artist,
those people at the next table, couples
at ease in their well-planned lives. Their timeshares
and yachts, his upset stomach, her headache.
All projection. I'm too much the witness.
Bring me another coffee and one more
piece of chocolate cake.
                      My earbud's dead.
          What am I
circling, what do we always
circle in the end? Apple tree, yew, hill
shrine? What do we circle when circling
the boundaries of our land? The central
lake stocked with trout?
                     We circle our parents.
We approach them down the road at sunrise.
They leap up, faces aglow, leap up
in the fresh breeze from the alder grove, all
purpose and faith, they leap round us.
           What we
approach in them comes back as a kind of
trust that will not unfurl in ten lifetimes,
no matter how long we circle or wait.
                     We wait
for our children, wait for them to approach
at sunrise, and when they come (they do not
always come) they dance up, faces aglow,
dance up in the fresh breeze, all purpose
and faith, they dance around us.

They lead us
toward childhood and leave us at the edge
of a dripping thicket.
                    The forgotten
in ourselves erupts: a rash on the chest,
an open book, one Christmas Eve, the tale
of a mother who so loved her son.

                    Catch
and release misses the moment. Holding
the fish in our arms is close as we come
to seasons, elements intersecting
in the middle of the gold citadel,
the fish still after the struggle, solid
strange pulseless epic quiescent still life.

With my father I fished the Roman Lakes,
maggot on hook on line spaced with lead spheres,
our bright cork floats signalling fish after fish,
our lines taut, silver droplets flashing down
the length of each perpetual autumn
afternoon connecting then and love to
a never patient bereft expanding
now, silver-taut, anxious and lifting.

IV

Increased pain in the groin after crossing the bridge to
Gatineau and back and roaming the National Gallery halls
and almost falling from a balcony into the courtyard with
spontaneous vertigo and inability to remember where I've been,
what I haven't seen.

> The difference
> Between Canada and England:
> Difference
> Between now and always

At Notre Dame blood in my mouth from the busted stitch
in the gum the dentist slit to see if the tooth was cracked (it
wasn't) adds to my fragility so I grab soup and bread and return
to the Arc and call home then taxi to The Barley Mow to lift
Sapporo and Molly from *The Beautiful Children* and receive a
magic silver ring.

> Four moveable bands
> Alphabet-stamped so
> You can make any
> Four-letter word so
>   Ring on ring on ring
> On ring on finger
> And Ottawa's gone
> Small family gone
> Vanished, disappeared
>   Is this where we start
> Or is it just me
> Cut from the sturgeon
> Cut from isinglass
> Fallen through the ice
>   Everything labelled
> Incomparable
> Ordinary life
> Found well, found new

V

Remember ghost towns where we were born, where we came
from, the voyage, first river view, promise of the new? The
sturgeon swam the same ghostly depths until it swallowed the
ring, the hook. Now is what revolves the rings of the ring? All
married to loss. Ghost women in fur coats offering pursed lips:
Goodbye! Goodbye! Goodbye!

Sapporo and Star feted, rooks and ravens aloft over the fallen
barley and first stars in the sky and new friends clinking glasses
over tabletops while brown river gods tumble over a changing
riverbed: *We'll miss you when you're gone but for now we'll
hold on.*

> What begins in water
> Continues in wood
> Continues in fire
> Continues in earth
> Continues in metal
> Returns to water

So many children in the spinning wind
pass round and round and pass again when change
and change turns the crank handle round again
with less and less resistance, each spiral
mashing grain fine and finer till
we reach the point of no resistance,
when each instance of gladness in us ends,
each instance of gladness, shame, and life ends,
and the rounds pass, rounds pass, also friends,
governors general, prime ministers, and
gulls, blown inland by the latest crazed storm,
wheel immodest, fevered, out of control
in the spinning wind, so many children.

Aftermath

The flow of moss
 Follows the flow of
  Water over rock

     Rock follows dirt
      The oldest fish stirs
       Before turning into a bird

The oldest bird follows
 The oldest sky
  The oldest word

    To hear what
       In the dry ditch
          Is waiting to rot

       The written word
        Divides spirit from soul
      Underfoot: tomorrow

        And yet still and still
          We can't read fragments
          Trying to surface

      Something big
    Won't ever be
   The way it is

Cut the grain
 It grows
  Again

Just fix
The invitation
List

Edward Elgar and guest
Gustav Mahler and guest
Charles Ives and guest

James Joyce and guest
Virginia Woolf and guest
Samuel Beckett and guest

Rainer Marie Rilke and guest
Carl Jung and guest
Thomas Stearns Eliot and guest

Hsie Ling-yün and guest
Lao Tzu and no guest
Chuan Tzu and

December 29th 2010

I Waited at Mallaig

Song

And if I want to love land, what better
land to love than this? And if I want to
love sky, what better sky to love than this?

Why circumscribe the day with to and fro?
Why travel all night to get somewhere else?

And if I want to love birds, what better
birds to love than these? And if I want to
love traffic, what better traffic to love?

The day she painted the fireplace white.
The day I biked in thirty degree heat.

And if I want to love bells, what better
bells to love than these? And if I want to
love a song, what better choir than this?

The night we slept with the window open.
All night long under the duvet.

Purchase

1.

On a ship at sea.
Enter Mariners.
Enter Mariners wet.

We're on the ferry to Victoria,
heads full of figures, dimensions and cash,
interest rates, lenders, amortization—

what a thing to sail toward, but Lorraine
is quick, her intuition unfettered
by fear, and fear's anxiety-coat slips

off my shoulders. Strange. How can entering
the world so emphatically not be
the terror predicted when I was born?

Offer accepted, papers signed, next week
the building inspection, ferry plying
black waves, I drift into a red green dream

that to enter harbour is pure terror
allayed only by dying or deep sleep,
our voyage a sleep, a sleep dreaming.

Perhaps sailing in and among others
is native to who we have always been.
What else belongs to a young man reading,

lighting the green fuse? The wake shrinks, edges
fade when he steps from one world to the next.
This is the way, the way, the wedding song

goes, the wedding song goes away, away.
To set sail gives us belonging and ease
from island to island, from sleep to sleep.

This is the way, the way, the wedding song
goes, the wedding song goes away, away.
The old prince unpacks stars and tides and books

and puts his dreams together again and
goes to sleep drunk, alone in a wheeled shack.
Who was it he loved? Where is his milk tooth?

The king on the hill, his father, will say
the queen has left with all the dappled mares
and will never know who she is or home.

2.

> *The island. In front of Prospero's cell.*
> *Lays down his robe.*
> *Enter Ariel.*

Remembered the bread and forgot the fruit.
Left it down below on the shoreline path.
Left it with the other stuff, just picked, ripe.

The bread and the jewel he remembered
to bring, remembered to bring for others
waiting for him with their own remembered.

All his cuffs were frayed, all his collars too.
Length and cut and fade of jeans looking good.
You are pushing your luck, me old boyo.

A voyage is a sleep; a sleep sailing,
dreaming in and among others perhaps
is native to who we have always been.

No, no. This is life after life, not death
after life. After Dyfi Junction and
the Cymru cuckoo—all change—remember

docking at Port Washington believing
this was America, a hundred owls
roosting the tree outside, a ghost on tip-

toe, hand gentle on your sleeping chest? *This
is your quiet dark green valley to bring
your parents to the end of days.* The ghost

as real as the hundred owls: *This is
the way, the way, the way we've always been
at the shipwreck of space and time and dream.*

3.

> *Another part of the island.*
> *Enter Ariel, invisible, playing solemn music.*
> *All sleep.*

No marriage, no ownership, no mainland,
no island, no house, no garden, no birds.
I found the seam on the roof of my mouth

after my tricksy mother tongue-kissed me.
Caliban in love seeks bisymmetry,
a single owl on the last hollow tree.

4.

> *Enter Caliban with a burden of wood.*
> *A noise of thunder heard.*
> *A man enters singing, a bottle in his hand.*
> *Drinks. Drinks. Gives Caliban drink.*

Riding the bus with St John of Salt Spring
who looks like John Mayall forty years on,
and businessman Bill, who has bought one son

a farm so he can go down and multiply,
and an airfield so he can get away
while his other son just writes poetry,

is surely a new poem on its way
to meet the building inspector, wherein
Bill tells us this other son will never

raise a family because there's no money
in poetry and *I can't imagine*
a more useless pursuit than poetry.

John asks Bill to name all his businesses
and Bill looks out of the window, *Is this*
the milk run? and opens his newspaper.

Bill says, *I'm going fishing,* and I say
there are things beyond money, and St John
gets serious, asks how long till my stop,

he has things to say, warn me about, wants
to pace himself. *Take Scientology,*
man. If you lose track reading, find the word

in the last paragraph that strikes you most
and dwell on it, dwell in it... He takes out
coins, *These are time,* and drops a penny

to the deck, picks it up and gives it me.
A loan with interest is betrayal;
a loan without forgiveness is the end

of us. He adds up Roman numerals
and shows me 666. *And they will use*
this time to pay the armies. Jesus was

a rich man, a perfumer who knew death
and only went into his father's house
for gold. Pay attention to the solving

and the warning... We are near my stop when
John of Salt Spring says, *This is not the end,*
it's neither the milk run nor the rapture,

this is father-to-son, saint-on-a-bus
map-making, and the poet must see all.
When I climb down from the double decker

and quit John's travelling church there's perfume
in the close dark of Douglas and Fort and
a black stone in my shoe. I cross the road

to the Royal Bank, deposit ninety
thousand dollars and take out ten, a tithe,
and ascend Fort Street to the promised land,

St John still going on about armies:
When men slay men we give them gold and land
to settle and hold... bones they must return...

Extraction

Another part of the island.
Enter Caliban and two others.
Enter Ariel, invisible.
Ariel plays the tune on a tabor and pipe.

In the waiting room, anxiety room,
Mum finds the inmates (her word) dangerous,
and what exactly are we doing here?
I need the toilet. I need the toilet.

Dad is waiting to have a tooth pulled out.
Okay. We'll go for a drive by the sea.
Okay. Then we'll pick him up and go home.
I need the toilet. I need the toilet.

You've got your work cut out, my father said,
she thinks we're putting her in a home.
He signs his name and goes in like a lamb.
His cousin OD'd in a dentist's chair

after the war while Dad waited for him
at Mallaig to go oversea to Skye
for rock climbing. Strike this out? Insert this?
Replace Dad with Prospero, Prospero

with Salt Spring John, Mother with Ariel,
the writer always Caliban? Pan back,
a little accordion vibrato
with clowns, fools, and recurrent melodies

for the end credits, and a coda? No.
An ache in the gut. An ache in the gut.
Ten thousand times I have to take my mum
to the public bathroom by the graveyard.

I hold my spooked mother's hand from the car
to the washroom, the crossings colder and
colder. *Where are we? Where is he? You will
find me when he's gone and look after me?*

Moaning across the street in the sea wind,
she will never manage alone, she can't,
simply can't, and this is a real nightmare…
But it isn't. It is just difficult.

*Can we go home? Where is he? Where is he?
I can never ever come here again!
Don't let me leave the island again. I
just want to go to sleep and not wake up.*

*People make such a fuss about death. It
is only death, a simple thing. This is
terrible, terrible. Where is he? Where's
your father? Where is he? Can we go home?*

*

As tricky as the whole extracted day,
he's drowsy on my arm, his mouth bloody,
goes to sleep in the back of the car
and Ariel settles, humming, in front.

We leave the orcas blowing the Milky
Way away between islands. Remember
that she won't remember. Dad must do that.
Remember that she won't remember that

you told her that she won't remember that
you told her that she won't remember that
you told her that she won't remember that
you told her that she won't remember it.

*

My father lost his eyetooth yesterday.
Over coffee I ask about Gordon's
death. He says, *I waited at Mallaig then
came home.* I ask him how is his socket?

His partial plate will not fit, the washing
machine is broken, he has edema
right ankle and foot, bruised and bleeding left
shin, and today his lungs are full and wet.

Who wrote Revelation? He doesn't think
John the Baptist. *Was it John the Prophet?
Was it John of Patmos?* He's not too sure.
Hence antibiotics for seven days.

*

A dead thrush by my garden gate. Tonight
a film festival by children with phones—
the last event on the island for me
is stop-motion Playmobil adventures.

All my frayed shirts will soon be thrown away.
Cuffs and collars will soon be clean and sharp.
All day precise things in precise order.
Nothing out of place. All buttons secure.

Mansion

In front of Prospero's cell.
Enter a man bearing a log.

My father has more space between his words,
more breath inside his lines, and his laugh is
the ironic answer to everything
now he is still alive at ninety-two
which starts to amaze even him. Only
death, island death, awaits his only life
while each day tilts, swerves, and accidents find
him half-dressed, besmirched, his colostomy
bag oozing on the carpet, and his wife,
my mother, absently robust upstairs.

I'm at sea approaching the big island,
disarray all round in currents and tides,
black sky scudding east, parents left behind.

On the long bike ride in from the ferry
I keep passing gloves, pointing or waving,
saying *halt*, saying *hopeless* and *go back*,
and realize that what I saw last night
in my mother's violent behaviour
besides stark fear was back-to-the-wall end
of autonomy. And I, first-born son,
will always be implicated, blamed and
forgiven, over and over again—

I trespass now as I trespassed then. Meant
the end of her long dream. Fought my father
for the raw margin she allowed the world.

Visitant

Solemn and strange music; and Prospero on the top, invisible.
Enter several strange Shapes, bringing in a banquet;
Ariel vanishes in thunder; then, to soft music, enter
the Shapes again, and dance with mocks and mows.

While he cooks, shops, recycles, remakes beds
others (enemies) have unmade at night,
Ariel invites the pigeons in, cuts
flowers and leaves, fills vases and wanders
room to room, brandy to brandy, hiding
underwear under the mattress. The world,

dying and memory start in a week,
when all history will face the mountain
that has no peak, no root. Ariel is
layered moment on moment, place on place,
always tuned to Prospero and not quite
yet, not yet, not all done with loving him.

I am almost my father's grandson but
for biology. When my mother wants
to use her tongue in a kiss it is time
to reframe ocean, land and sky, living
arrangements. If he is sky and she land,
I must be ocean. Ariel gets it,

then doesn't. More and more often doesn't.
These are their final days. *Good Prospero,*
she says. And he says, *Today's not so good.*
She doesn't know me and wants to go home.
I am almost my father's father but
for biology. When my mother wants

to reframe ocean, land and sky, living
arrangements, I must be pacific. I
get it. I know she's eaten nothing and
been drinking since morning; she knows me but

not my father, quizzes him on their past
to catch him in a lie, confesses all,

early lovers, trysts their marriage covered,
says her memory is not the best. *Who
are you? Who else is here?* He will not raise
his head. *Just our son*, he says, *no one else.*
We are in a painting of a cottage
not one of us will ever recognize.

Genomic Archaeology

A noise of hunters heard. Enter divers Spirits in shape
of dogs and hounds, hunting them about; Prospero
and Ariel setting them on.
Caliban and men are driven out.

On deck between the cafeteria
and the forward lounge: outside a remnant
of where we used to live, now a passage
from room to room, inside to inside,
with a chilled view of lit clouds, volcano,
a forest of cranes above coal barges,
acres of sea: the metal shine of things
later forgotten; islands in the strait
still later named, the flip-side lately lost,
and finally the cafeteria,

the forward lounge, and finally the depths,
the exploration of prehistory
and the mining of bloodlines that leads me
to this valley, these trees, from clear pursuit
(the cheetah catches the slowest pronghorn),
leaves out all those who refuse to tremble,
who don't make mistakes, who give false readings,
those who shed others' blood, build churches on
temples, temples on barrows, those who map
emptiness and successfully evolve.

They Sold the Truth

Ariel aside to Prospero.
Prospero aside to Ariel.
Ariel aside to Prospero.
Prospero aside to Ariel.

A month after we moved uphill to Fort
they sold the Truth Centre across the street
and flushed the stag into morning traffic.

Setting out to see my parents one more
last time I passed the stag and we marvelled
at each other and dreamed death by falling.

They buried us beneath a rotting log
in an autumn forest and winter came,
then spring, and my parents lived on and on.

Our bones grew wide and filled with stars under
the mossy spore-filled trunk and my parents'
house sailed quiet evenings—fir, maple,

arbutus, fir, maple, arbutus, fir—
until the Truth Centre's Garry Oaks were
furniture passed through six generations,

a future child was found inside an oak
chest with the photo of a stag startled
from a grove of trees. Once upon a time.

Holes

Aksara

The deathless death place, small efforts of life,
the idea of bliss and bliss itself,
the idea of birth—not birth—replaced
with light, *I am that witness of water*

pristine, pure, still, beginningless: this end,
these clear words, these even scattered letters,
what is or was or will be, unknown not
known, nothing left undone, nothing unsaid,

no one left to turn off the gas and light,
secrets you wanted to tell simply told.
The pigeons for a few generations
fly window to window begging seed from

the empty dreaming house. The heron stilts
the stagnant pond. Ghost goldfish swim below.

Ghosts

spun a web about the house, drained the well
spun a web about the house, filled the well

To The Ferry

I have just learned there are holes, lacunae
where things looked pretty firm, solid, stable.

My sister is not my father's daughter.
She swabbed his cheek and hers, compared results.

I spat in a tube, spat and spat, compared
my result to hers and found I am

my sister's brother, our dad is childless,
our father killed himself in England.

I watch a young grey nun at the bus stop
reading the schedule, darkness before dawn

almost total, when contemporary
bucolics, a devil and apprentice

in rags, cross between us: *Opposition,
see?* says the devil. *A lamb of God, see?*

Essss—stupid—esss! quoth the youth weaving
by me in the street, wafting aftershave.

On the bus John of Salt Spring is preaching
from the lower deck as dawn pinks Baker,

false prophet extolling, aggregating
disciples from the sleepy travellers.

Agnus the lamb of God is in the dock
when I arrive at the north carrying

peppercorns from our mother's land to seal
the holes before the splinters of darkness

can cross the field of light before the waves
can kiss the island shore. Each peppercorn

is a planet of extinct volcanoes
or a happy-go-lucky comet; when

each carves a track through unfathomable
energy, its pull, many-located,

misunderstood, is not yet here, not now,
now in my shoe, now back in my pocket.

On the Long Bike Ride

A man in a suit sleeps under a tree
curled between great roots. Birds begin to sing.

So many ways they have of sending you
back into the fray. Mend you. Patch you up.

A buck is poised astride the yellow line
facing south by the farm I used to own.

Why are you not in uniform? And why
are you not in bed? Winter is shining...

How did we get here? How will we survive?
Surely this is complete, impossible.

all the way here from the Belgian front.
Look up tonight, boys, at the harvest moon

A salamander starts across the road
as the October light begins to fail

that was waxing when we were together.
It's been a slice but I can't cut it (ha!)

and she curls on my palm at the dull heat
(dark on top, orange beneath). I help her,

across—so long, Dad, so long, Mum, so long,
girls and boys, this is the merry-go-round.

the salamander, half across the road
as the October light begins to fail.

The music has stopped, time to get off
the wheel, road, tree, branches, twigs, leaves, sky, stars...

I also curl, heart clenching in the night
(dark on top, orange beneath). I help her.

So many ways they have of sending you
back into the fray. Mend you. Patch you up.

Each is isolated in the moment
of her being, complete, impossible.

Refugee

the strangest thing about this life this time
to come home to find the broken mended

and no sign of how this might have been done
mother in the kitchen cooking

a single giant mushroom and dad
building a fire for the coming night

sister by the window singing
both sets of grandparents dreaming

with all the ancestors and villagers
with all the ancestors and villagers

both sets of grandparents dreaming
sister by the window singing

building a fire for the coming night
a single giant mushroom and dad

mother in the kitchen cooking
and no sign of how this might have been done

to come home to find the broken mended
the strangest thing about this life this time

Attraction

We met in darkness, almost total truth,
close to joy, at a basement bar amid

a late crowd, small schools of threes and sevens.
She finned the silt beside me and we kissed.

In daylight she is young, I am nearly
old. She will leave me any minute now,

any minute now she'll leave me, I am
that much in love. *Oh what a fool,* she says.

*

Ignorance swims away. It is fear.
They say the country of fish is too deep.

Eggs flower, explode, our fry seed the sea.
I build a wall all heart, she breaks it down.

In the rock pool the reflected moon is
wind rippled, in love with recognition.

So crazy. Why should muscle penetrate
fire? They say truth is here for all to see.

Traction

I'm at my parents' house with my sister,
documents strewn across the living room
floor, the stream meandering all the way

to England, over Hadrian's wall north
to Scotland and no cities, only hills,
distant crags and outcroppings, the wide road

rising gently beside the beck into
white matted flying cloud on a winter
morning turning west, a thin sheet of ice

over the tarmac, the luxury bus
with rooms and storage must travel slowly,
the driver says, this journey is risky

(we're sure this journey is *very* risky)
and outside the windows are outcroppings
and crags that turn into, no, *are*, ancient

buildings hewn out of or superadded
to the original igneous rock,
molten a moment ago, the buildings

once-fine mansions, imposing temples, now
dead, bleak, empty, beginning to crumble
by the side of the vast descending road.

*

Another passenger, a man, presses
his hand to my head, removes a layer
of skin, a ring of bone, to see inside.

I cannot speak or react or question,
only lie down and realise he is
merely an adolescent boy of twelve,

our young father who killed himself before
we knew who he was (not the man who raised
us, married our mother, kept that secret),

a boy who gives me news of who I am,
my sister's brother, not our father's son
and at Mallaig we witness ignorance

dispelled as the clouds are from the distant
cliffs of Skye, and the ferry docks to take
us there across the glass-still waveless sea.

Quartet: The World Speaks to the Stars

1.

The windows contained green hills, rippled and
distorted. The children dressed in rain capes
squeaked along the blue tiles. Their son struggled
with the sprung bathroom door. Lunch would be soon.

*The clock is damaged and will take eight weeks
to repair,* he said. *I didn't notice
it had stopped,* she said. The room froze.
Their conversation was unlike human

conversation. More like birds calling. Like
ravens. Incredible. *I'm in two rooms
at once,* he said. *I'm between lives,* she said,
and set fire to her belly. It will take

them the rest of their lives to wake from this.
They won't know time, and the world, uncontained,
will spark, splinter, burn and start to collapse.
Where will we go? she said. *To sleep,* he said.

2.

Now Europe has burned, now America,
now the tall capitals of Asia and
the Middle East stagger between old sky,
new desert, it's time to look past the fault

lines of books and marketplaces, nightmare
carbon forests, the thousand-bone berm, to
Africa and beneath Africa to
the seismic foundation of sea-sorrow.

3.

4.

The holes will fill
The water will be blue
The land green

Emerald in a blue setting
Island in the middle
Reeds, ducks, canoes

Cypress Hills

Over the Rockies flying east, smooth ride,
smooth white, then towers of cloud and devils
dancing under the wings, and stomach ache,
anxiety just at bay, sky turquoise
fields, black shadows and the Train of Terror,
rain squalls west, and north brilliant blue with
slow shunting cumulus cars over flax,
middle of here and now to Cypress Hills
where we pitch tents at the equestrian
campsite and eat veggie burgers and talk
about the people who found this place
at the beginning of the world and wove
dreams into the grass on the dry hilltops
in September and watched the glacier
slide by. Rain on the tent roof. Tarp spilling
rain, then a rain walk. Did I say rain? Rain
rolling off the plateau with the gumbo,
rain slopping one hour into steady
yellow-green and grey, great big continents
slipping overhead, scrims on pulleys, God's
raiment, many shades—these bumpy bits born
of the Rockies in their teens and shaved by
streams and rivers a long way from any
ocean now, my friends, till we travel back

west toward the invisible mother,
threatening all day, falling all night. No
contact with the outer world, in fact no
outer world. What was outer is outer
no longer. All is inside. When we die
we will know what we leave is on the edge
of catastrophe, but is this any
different from what our mother's father's
mother knew? All are afraid of what will
come after the fact of desire and birth.

Cold, with a half moon and no wind. After
dark the fire in the iron monopod
is useless to keep a body warm and
the excellent scotch is insufficient,
and pleasant conversation and cigars
give way to swift retirement to our tents.

Minus 5 morning, pancakes and maple
syrup with black scotch and the small cigars
we like, then up the Trans-Canada Trail
to the plateau where we munch fruit candies
and watch a circling hawk watch us circle
the conglomerate cliffs and back to camp
for Black Bridge IPA, bagels, lox and
Danish blue, more black scotch, afternoon nap.

I am a deposit from old seas that
water has worked for millennia. View?
Grass hills and swathes of coniferous woods,
green trees yellow at the edges, a moon
tunnel in dark-tinged grey cloud, wind shifting,
memory, imagination, friendship,
instability, pain, illness—who else
is the mother of the deposits? What's
the deposit, what's the mother? Always

return west, assume death, always moment
and transition. Snow. Crosses. The. Highway.
Each shelterbelt proclaims each dynasty,
far-flung to a coastal eye, on ridges,
tucked into gentle folds in the brown hills,
in truth rather more like barrows than hills.

What does the inkblot spread on the notebook
say at ten thousand feet above mountains,
clouds like great grey badgers drinking the lakes?
How did we tease particles of light from
the darkness? How carry a million
years of debris a thousand miles? Why is
this blonde woman offhand and disdainful,
when her eyes show vulnerability
and an old, childish, learned self-consciousness?
Her bearing as she retreats down the aisle
is glacial, stately, Russian. Ashblonde
hair covers half her long nape and mountains
outside the window give way to brown hills
and the purpose of imagination:
to transform what is light and dark into
the tried and true ritual of the sun.

The purpose of memory is to keep
alive such sacraments in blind glory.
We will not look into shadow by day
because it contains nothing, but we know
by night it defines the world in terror.

The woman is night come into daylight.
She raises old questions and fading self-
belief. The light and dark strands of her hair
swing gently like silk bell ropes as she glides
away down the aisle and the plane staggers
through turbulence, silk strands reveal a long
riddle of grey stone to either side and
below the fuselage as we descend.

Pacific, that

for the first heaven and the first earth were
passed away; and there was no more sea.

Revelation 21:1

I

A young man reading power, naming the leaves picked off the deck,
forges belonging on another day of no rain, tastes words,
tastes names, forges the present so memory is freewheeling
and family shame redundant, *and the gears do not engage.*
It was in my hand and I did not remember writing it.
The past is a fog, the young man prideful, he is in me yet.

On a single-client Wednesday, I rode my bike home to find
Lorraine was at the memorial of her first husband, Mark,
murdered at sunset on Kits Beach. The client thought she hadn't
needed to come, came anyway and said she found in writing
dreams the space she needed to grieve her only son, gone last year.
Overdose deaths, personal deaths. Mark. Bill. Iain. The nib sweats.

Adjo sleeps inside on his chair, his eyelid cracked; Luna sleeps
outside—lovely cats but I know death is all, around us all,
every day it's done, all done. Saying to Dad and Mum the air
is so still, the trees so still—so tame, it's terrible really.
The past is a fog, the young man prideful, he is in me yet—
I wait for you to start your solo. Are you there? Here is mine.

*

August last year the days were going the way they'd always gone
and I was still at the pad with a pen wanting a line, this
line, any line, this one, then Bill was dead. Catastrophic stroke
with heart attack. Lorraine's dad Bill, first of our four past the post.

They do that, interrupt each other. As the days wandered by
I distracted myself, self-stimming, but the absence of sex
was the problem needed solving. I got it one day between
the bathroom and living room. *Realization.* What was it?

Something to do with the illicit: sex must be transgressive.
That simple. I just needed to break the contract between sex
and death. Steveston would do. Where Bill died is where the river
meets the sea and industry meets tourism. Pacific that close.

Losing words, chasing words in the beer, must practise, run 'em down.
Four Chinese girls walk between two pubs to the tea-brown river.
I drink Fat Tug and speak to the waitress. Four Indian girls
stride into the village, laughing. Other words are locked away.

I am in Steveston and Lorraine is on the island. Murdered
husband, dead dad. Out of mention, I am alive. It's like this
on a late summer Friday night when a father dies. *Symbol.*
Fish frying interrupts gasoline. Call off the search. We're done.

October. Begin with the definite article, make it
the humility of belonging. Systems aside, every
position occupied, we must return to meaning and the
temporal thrust, go with gut impulse before counter-impulse,
or hold our tongue, hang fire, stand at the back of the room, outside
the forest, in the burbs before they are burbs, fin de siècle,
that breathless instant after the mash-up tune-up, before the
conductor lifts his baton—language open for translation.

Quiet woman, quiet man. Every hundred years an
indestructible couple. Tone of voice washed down
the generations to speak here, intent understood,
details lost. This must be the way ghosts live
in our world. These must be ghosts. I speak for
the living, though these days I hang with those
who've surrendered that status. There are circles
of ghosts, and here, overlooking the strait
and islands, the ghosts fit within our ranks.

November. Disordered mind. Disrupted present.
End of days. Revelation on an island fortress. Close
within the narrow world ghosts and a single hole—
rat hole.

Lorraine brought the camera bag down from the studio and
inside was my old Nikon SLR with 35mm and 85mm lenses,
canisters of undeveloped film and English coins, detailed map
of New York City, iron rail spike, *Duino Elegies*, *The Sonnets
of Orpheus*, the *Pocket Tao Reader*, Stephen Mitchell's
Tao te Ching. Oh, and a bamboo ink brush set and a screwdriver set.

Do you need all this? Can you sell it? Will it go to the Nu-To-You?
What I did was pretty good. I used Bill's car to take a bag of garbage
to the dump, an expired propane cylinder to the fire station,
empty beer bottles to the depot, I repaired the English
Waterman's silver safety that belonged to D.T. Stephens,
listened to Steve Lacy and Mal Waldron. It was the most
beautiful winter day, everything glittering. Then I listened

to ISIS *Nashids*, those *Nashids* young Muslims would hear
on the battlefield or at executions, to normalize daily life.

December brought the new edition of
an old dream of *travelling with my dad*
to a wild English place near rushing falls
where he and my mother were young again
and he was wearing a close-fitting felt
hat and leaping along the river path.
I reached out to save him from falling and
we both lost our balance. In the water
I was sure of death (how easy to say).
Banks I reached for crumbled and we were swept
past gratings beyond which we saw people
shopping under bright lights, another world.
We would transfer ourselves there. I could do
this, I was drowning to write down the dream.

I woke not so free as when I was free
as a child exiled. A Spy in Exile.

III

Lorraine's birthday is the beginning of February
and this year she is sixty and Bowie's gone and
we buy *Dark Star* from Lyle's, then walk to Value
Village to buy a kettle and Rebecca West's *Black
Lamb and Grey Falcon*, and Ashlan phones while

we are browsing trinkets. Her son has remembered.
Midnight might be food poisoning, might be the
weekend away, but between falling asleep—avoiding
other skaters around the rink—and waking is
a night as long as a life or as Balkan history.

＊

At the Rosedale on Robson I am a captain,
hands on the wheel, quite confident of
sleep, and the journey's end is Microsoft
beside a stadium, sky fangs down sky.
It comes light and pigeons fly the fangline.

A man on the roof, two checking the vents.
Technique and Love. Evolution and Failure.
After a breakfast of coffee and croissant—
thinking of asking my brother-in-law, which
is worse, the cancer or the serial losses owing

to plaques and tangles? but not asking, already
knowing that loss and silence are making him
lonely. He is planning, he tells me, always planning
a solo life. His mother pushed away forever those
she deemed had betrayed her. We part company.

All floods back in reflection: False Creek pilings, boats
at rest, water at rest, geese launching off Harbourside
under Cambie's steel and concrete smudge. A man
in a red jacket asks the time: one single dark clouded
hour before the noon train to see Margaret, Bill's widow.

IV

March. Waterman's Black Silver Overlay.

The death I write away from, my several hand-
writings at war, just wants to tell a plain story.
Forbidding ghosts. The main character a boy, no
doubt about it. Secondary: a girl. Also
no doubt. A burst of joy. Put on the old duffel,
hood up, and leave the old life behind. Winter flood.
A drip from the roof onto the foot of the bed
on an evening at the trailer away from home.
On the edge of brilliance but not brilliant,
out of joy. Writing until the ink runs out.

An Otter

An otter has crawled from the wavelets to die on the beach. To
die on his belly in the arms of a drift-log, rear paws out,
pads open to the sky, front claws reaching, nose turned east,
eyes and mouth gently closed. The spring sun has not unmade
him yet or begun to. This is a quiet bay. The log felled and
limbed long enough ago to bleach, dry to the core, is
his head-cross and Lorraine's stride-perch. She cries out when
she steps over and sees him dead, asleep, asleep, dead.

There is no smell. The sun has not touched him yet.
He only just got here. He is only old. He came here for this.
Brown fur dark along the spine, still glossy.

Prairie, this

there should be time no longer...
the mystery of God should be finished

Revelation 10:6, 7

I

A young man reading the green fuse. The way things shrink
to the edges when you shill from one room to the
next, one world to the next. This is the way, the way
the wedding song goes, the wedding song goes away.

April. What must I do now? I'm still plying sea
among islands, entering Active Pass over
and over, the old round, a transit a thousand
generations old, three wives old this time around.

(the islands record me!) (the waves!) (my fair lady.)

Use up ink. Enough ink so that the vest pocket
safety will not leak on the plane tomorrow as
I gain altitude. I'm travelling east, let's say,
2016. Ancestors marched east to fight Crusades.

Should they survive the battles, the march, what would be
left? Who would return? What would they do? I'm leaving
Lorraine on our anniversary to go write
at Wallace Stegner's childhood home in Eastend (once

Whitemud) in a bend of the Frenchman River,
in a valley once bay to a wooded island
in the inland sea, once the tongue of an ice edge.
A beach. A shallow fishing lagoon. Yes, perhaps.

And those prints in the mud? Left by beasts cutting
white clay tablets for laws. (John the Divine, of course!)
Meanwhile Cicely and I consider Germans
of the thirties as latest versions of the Goths

who spoiled the Romans' Western Empire song and dance
and now suffocate under bureaucratic silt,
not able to understand simple equity
and truth, yet able to see and remark beauty.

II

Why did I think I needed a shoelace? I found one
in my shaving kit. Talk doesn't do it, nor snow fence,
nor trucks crossing on a gravel road. (Meadowlark?)

I walk into someone else's house. (Raven.)
I walk into someone else's house. (Bluebirds.)
I walk into someone else's house. (Stegner's.)

The picket I propped the gate open with snapped,
such is the aridity (a word Seán uses, eschews, uses),
and now the gate swings in the wind.

Ah, Gentleman Jack, how will you begin?
With a dream by the river, a promise
of lignite and a section of fat wheat.

The weather was hot when I arrived and then the wind
blew and blew: chairs flew across the brown cone-covered
lawn, the gate yawed, while I watched from the study

the local trees and dry stubble and stick brush frantic
for attention, and then the temperature dropped and
it snowed, and this was Southern Saskatchewan early

April. A hundred writers have written
from this upstairs view, out of the house built
a hundred years ago by George Stegner

for his family, so they could over-winter,
the homestead south too harsh, isolated,
"weathering and rusting and blowing away."

The river runs at the bottom of the garden,
on the other side of the alley, meanders around
Whitemud, flows to the Milk, to the Missouri.

1875 three hundred North-West Mounted Police
trundled their way west across those hills—the sage-
green pillows the Assiniboine Cree wove to get from

unnamable place to unnamable place—from
Wood Mountain to Fort Walsh, and I hereby
unname the stations again from my vantage place.

He that is unjust, let him be unjust still: and
he which is filthy, let him be filthy still: and
he that is righteous, let him be righteous still: and

he that is holy, let him be holy still. (Rev. 22:11)
Now I'm really afraid. I have never
wanted to face anything directly

and now I face these hills, white-clay line that
tells of the old ocean bed, so the stone-
layer said to me across the iron

bridge when I visited his house, dream of
a dead wife, fox with a brace of robins.
Facing the fox indirectly is the way

to the numinous prairie. This is the
mouth, do not ever look at the eyes. Lips
will tell you all you want to know. Eyes show

she is already elsewhere, with her pups.
Mother at Halloween is hurt when I
come between her and the trick-or-treaters.

She looks beyond Dad before crouching to
leap away. This room faces west, I should
have guessed, and morning sun colours the fields.

Not fields, that's just an expression. Hills? Yes.
Such words belong to childhood and this room
was childhood for the Stegner boys. What is

happening to me is what happens when
sun beats into the room at sunset and
sweat trickles down your back. I look forward

into the weeks of my stay because I'm
by nature solitary and the paths
over those hills go nowhere. That story

requires ground and revelation. Where
will I go, I would like to know, and what
will happen? Is there a lost battlefield?

Is there a wolfer still roaming among
dead and dying horses this windy spring
afternoon? This is not right. It moves me,

but if there's a battlefield and horses
are dying why would he flog even one
of them? Far from home, he beats the horses

because they are his, because he loves them.
Blood on the hills. Seventy grizzles killed
in a day. Countless buffalo, coyotes.

III

The lips, not the eyes, lips not eyes. But eyes
carry hills into the room. In the past
this was the shallow bay of an island.

The car that drove me here was driven by
a hawk and I have vestigial gills.
A housefly waited in the house. Lady-

bug. Seán and I drove south from Saskatoon,
exhausted, talking, then quiet. Father
fills Mother's eyes. He is all. And I cry

at my sister's name. None of us have gone
away. None of us have gone away. None.
Lorraine and Ashlan. My maps and note-

books. A wasp on the carpet disintegrates
into segments when I pick it up. Head,
thorax, legs. Black-and-white cats cross the yard,

scratch the stump and stretch every late
afternoon as I talk to Lorraine and drink beer.
Stewart climbs from his truck, walks bowlegged

to the steps, to his door, and the journey
takes millennia. A red tabby joins
a black-and-white on the old man's roof.

He pushes his walker down the front steps
and strolls Tamarack to Handel, largo,
in new jeans, bright buckle, green ball-cap.

Nightfall I go out into the silent white dust
behind the house and find a small river
and a bridge to the ridge, a spine, and meet

an arthritic dog. Old gal is only eight—
they age quickly here. Where is my voice
to talk to these people, their dogs and cats?

Toil uphill with the idea of climbing out,
out of the valley, but the dust blown up by
the odd truck spins me back, black boots grey.

Let me see if I can find out what I am.
(Eat an apricot every second day.)
A hundred years ago this was a town

and two trains a week connected Whitemud,
cattle ranches and other start-up towns
to the outside world. Whiteface mill among

buffalo ghosts twice-weekly, suspended
above the grassland in a miasma
all the way from here to the Cypress Hills.

*

Wallace's dad won the lot in a non-
stop poker game played in Joe Knight's hotel
until it burned down, then Christenson's pool-

hall (the town's fifteen kids at school upstairs),
until the hotel was rebuilt. Ghosts still
play below the kids doing morning sums.

Boys hunted like Habsburgs from 2 to dusk.
Jewish, Syrian, Greek Orthodox and
two Chinese families lived in Whitemud.

"For the isolates, there were only two
alternatives: join or be excluded."
The Syrian family of nine fit in.

The house was built following the 1915
bumper wheat crop. Pure shadowless mid-
war opportunity. Wallace was six. He slept

in this room till he was eleven when
the family quit and crossed into Montana.
They slept a last night in the boarded-up

shack before shutting the gate, heading south,
"hooking shut three strands of barbed wire around
the place we had made there... such a tight, firm fence."

When he was sixty-three (my present age)
he won the Pulitzer for *Angle of Repose*.
In 1963 when I was ten, he was walking

the hills and wetlands of the San
Francisco peninsula ("Something will have
gone out of us as a people if we ever

let the remaining wilderness be destroyed...")
and I was awarded my Crusader
Knighthood Bible, which sits on the corner

table bookmarked to John's *Revelation*.
...give him a white stone, and in the stone
a new name written, which no man knoweth... (*Rev.* 2:17)

*

A lion, a calf, a man
and an eagle, six wings
apiece, full of eyes, restless.

Open the book (double-edged steel-tongue)
amid the animals, the lamb just killed
with seven horns, seven eyes. A white horse.

Not good
to eat bad shit or fuck indiscriminately.
Jezebel or Babylon.

Open the book. Time ends.
Three chairs at the picnic table, one thrown
back by the wind; two of me calm, the third

shocked. A white horse and a warrior king.
A red horse and a warrior general.
A black horse and a measuring scale.

A pale horse pulling a cart of corpses.
Open the book. The dead awaken and
the world ends (the map folded up).

Consciousness ends; the star falls.
Horse-locusts with human masks.
Open the book.

(I raise my pen to write.)
Time ends.
A girl is looking for a place to birth

her child because her water has broken.
In her path a monster waits to eat the child.
When I was born a monster drew me out.

I couldn't find my mother for days.
The wine press, the blood. Everything
forgotten in tangles and lesions except

her sixteenth year when everything
happened, all at once. Every genesis, every
truth, every lie.

(A barking dog. Steady gusts.)

(RAPTURE)

*

Seán and I drive west out of the valley,
step into wind you can lean on and hold
up and step on barbed wire so we can walk

down into a long draw, a slender cut
in the prairie that has in it bluebirds,
that has in it hawks, a small herd of deer,

pools of yellow snow, rattling thorn bushes,
a petrified branch, the bones of a stag,
tip of one antler he shows me nibbled

by a porcupine. This is the hawk man.
This is the shaman. This is the father.
The bones are ones I've seen on a cave wall.

✻

London Bridge is falling down falling down
Grip the hundred year Waterman's safety,
nib extended, between my teeth. Jasper,

sapphire, chalcedony, emerald.
Fresh water from the German co-op girl
(impressive black eye, full-sleeve tattoos done

in Medicine Hat a third the cost of
Berlin tats) and it's 1916 again,
midnight bell, crashing through the bell Tower

in Ottawa, clangs again in Whitemud.
Eliot and Stegner, listen to me,
listen to that wind, that ringing. *Build it*

up with wood and clay, wood and clay, wood and...
George Stegner made $27.15
cultivating, hoeing. Listen to that

wind, that bell. *Wood and clay will wash away...*
wind will scatter filthy dreams, clouds without
water, pluck up trees whose fruit has withered.

Rootless, I had many things to write but
because I no longer know my name and
cannot face-to-face greet friends by name

bricks and mortar will not stay, will not stay.
The pen in my mouth, gold nib extended
will not stay. Bricks and mortar will not stay,

is a dummy, a nipple, a blade of grass,
will not stay, will not stay, my fair lady,
I can't take out, I won't take out, I can't.

Iron and steel will bend and bow bend and
(I can't stay in, I won't stay in, I won't)
baby, it's cold outside, baby it's cold.

People asking what am I working on.
Baking cookies, reading *Revelation.*
Pigeon on the wire, beak into the wind,

tail working like a derrick, heart riffing.
The jet trail fat as a spooked cat's tail
a half hour past sunset. My chapbooks:

Winter Wedding, Broad Street Blues, Ottawa,
sit with the Bible, glasses and a pen,
for me to read while I'm here writing this.

You want to sit profoundly at the edge
of an inland sea, the women who you
carry to carry you, to all be there?

What of them? What is the sense to a sea
circled by men? A woman circled by
land? The presence or absence of water?

IV

Light just hold us, hold us against
          darkness.
The joining planned so long is
          beginning
with grizzly ghosts in the Cypress Hills,
rifle stock slotted between the left arm
and the chest wall. Sun striated through trees.

These are the atria, these ventricles.
Breath just hold us, hold us against
          dying
light when colour in the lodge poles
          lingers
and the bears and lions show themselves.

What are you afraid of most? Some say cats,
others bears. I only want to pen two brilliant
stark-as-the-day-is-long-as-the-crow-flies lines.

Who am I? How did I get here? What is
the itinerary? How can we go on? Can we go on?
Woman. Man. We cannot see our own.
Death just hold us, hold us against
          brightness.
It is coming—no thing stands in the way. Not
the photograph of the weeping tree
          true
to its place. Not the collared dove, scourge-
          survivor.
Let there be a camera. Let there be a recording
so we can identify all the people
we are and have been.

Lord of animals, will the sun ever
shine on the north side of my house?

Lord of animals, Lorraine and I wait
all morning in the east room, all
evening in the upper west room
to meet the sun and are disappointed
only by clouds. Lord of animals, shall I
build my house open to the north or
south, east or west?

Lord of animals, a storm hits and passes so fast.
        No time.
Nothing of what I wanted to say
is what I can say now.
We're just waiting for the first
familiar chord when we should
be listening for the modulation.

Lord of animals, all my shirts have ragged cuffs.

("but poetry sings past even the sadness
that begins it," sings Galway Kinnell)

In the brain of the brain the poem is still going.
You can hear it muttering all the words it can
remember, all the fragments that start over
as soon as finished to see if it can remember
another fragment and instead a church gathers
out of a churchyard and a grave opens
out of a field, flowers as far as the eye
can see on either side of the path a girl
has made gathering bluebells in a meander;
her mother loved these flowers, said they
were her poems, but only in a vase
in the piano window.

v

When Alfred Redl sees the Kaiser in the park
(a grave brooding figure facing the snowy valley,
guards at a practised disinterested distance)
as he passes in a carriage with Kubanyi's sister,
he laughs, so delighted is he in his life.

When I revise old poems the purpose
is to uncover the tracks between the trees—
there beneath the fallen snow—
pure conceit to believe that new words
can spoil the old ones. There is a path

the Kaiser was trying to make out,
to remain on or to deviate from,
and it had to do with Germany and
Austria-Hungary and should he forget
himself and fall to his knees or all fours.

The story is perhaps in bipedal footprints or
on the wing, or a finned flash eons ago,
but it is the story that matters; the words
are just for grace and balance. Lying
on my back, eyes wide open, looking

straight up into the blue blue sky,
I see three birds directly above:
two hawks facing each other and
a smaller bird between them. All
equidistant, hovering, wings poised, all

attending to the still moment,
all in a dream; but the left hawk is
in a deep trance with the small bird,
while the right hawk begins to
close the distance. I know what is

going to happen. The smaller bird
will die; there are mouths to feed.

*

Across the river, beyond the singing meadowlark,
is a tall green shed with a red roof and no door.

A small flock of pigeons flies about the trees,
about the shed, wings clapping, white Vs, some

grey, and it must be a cote because a man
stands a long time under the bare branches,

barely green with buds sky-lined. I for him
must be a seated river figure half

up the far bank the water has taken
a long time to carve. I have noticed that

people here stand and look or sit and look
and look for a long time. In the city

they would be deemed unengaged,
homeless or crazy. These watchers, like

Colonel Redl's Kaiser, observe the flock
wheeling. The river divides the two men.

*

Wind. Not able to grasp what's in front
because wind and land are only sensible
to the robins and meadowlarks.

Dryness. Intelligence of the past in
a lump of grey coral, a crenellated brain
I find on the hillside. I came here to find

the boy and find coral. I came to find
the boy and find the river and the boy
at every turn. I came for sea and find sea.

There were plaques and tangles and
I find plaques and tangles. There was
forest and I find forest. There was ice

and I find ice. There were dogs barking
and I find dogs. There were flags flapping
and I find flags. But everything is unsteady,

unstable, though it seems at a glance
not so. Everything comes at you like
a coyote, like the full moon, like a fox,

from any direction. The surrounding ridge
spins all things down into the valley
and all things spiral around the people.

VI

D'Annunzio in Fiume and Donald Trump
in Colorado share their thoughts in a dream.
Waterboarding, by all means, and other
tortures too. The superman wills it. After
all, the monsters are just *over there*
and they are cutting our heads off.

I move my black gloves from the arm
of the burgundy couch to the morning porch.
Just settling in before leaving. Being
stalwart. Unless I stick like cactus to
the sole of a boot. I have owned this room
where Wallace and his brother went to

sleep and woke up for childhood years.
To grasp where I am I try a 360 on
the hillside, but cannot hold the view
or any particular of the scene, a slow
360, and I hear the word *Split* and think
of *The Tempest*, of Dalmatia. Do

another revolution and time slips.

VII

As if to fight what is coming, stock-
piling deaths to come—what else can I do,
the deaths are attaching like lampreys to

my lungs—I write *I'm by nature solitary*,
I'll find the theme later, before I go.
The days are hot. I dream our young Adjo

falls over the deck and into the bush,
my parents come for gin and tonic.
The frightening edges of life are still

at bay, though in Saskatoon weeks ago
I saw Canavan's backyard before spring.
I do not understand the dry wind, where

it comes from, what's in it. The streets are wide
as empty dreams, all is a dream of death.
But surely that can't be. I have been stopped

by magic ways of saying then grown bored
then discovered familiar formations
and found the land in words (without land).

I tried to copy the spells and ways of
casting and stole a little magic by
using the words, but words no longer held

the world. They don't hold the world because we
absorb the shallow fast first meaning, which
is all reflection, sky and bridge and moon

in water. (Use the spell to go deeper.)
The mind's absorption of the reflection
has its own reflection, and this means the

end of words, the end of word's flesh—the end
of land. When I arrived in Stegner's house
I bounded up and down the thirteen stairs,

with coffee, water, empty dishes and
books, and got used to the funhouse effect.
Now I'm about to leave, the snow won't stop.

If we are not written into the book
we are in the lake of fire. I am
no lamb to write names and have no seal-key.

When I arrived in Stegner's house I read
somewhere in John's *Revelation*: *And time
ended*. A single verse. Time ended.

Now I find no such verse. 10:6 says there
will be time no longer, but that's to come.
Time ended. I read it in my Bible,

the one I got when I was ten. And yet
time did not end. There was no tempest. There
was no Split. No wreckage of the cities.

The two boys who shared this room only want
to fly the landing, down the thirteen stairs,
sling their bodies around the banister, through

the kitchen, slip on shoes and .22s,
out the back door, beat you to the river.
I realize that time has not ended

and bake chocolate cookies, chocolate chocolate
chip, batch after batch, to fill the thing that
time has left and put away death for a bit.

Time has not ended but reversed. Time's end
has found me time-reversed. Hawk and poets
leave me in a blizzard at summer's start.

*

Anna Livia Plurabelle, was she
pike in the Whitemud, Irishman fishing?
Malloy, is that yourself, boyo? No, it's

imagine dead imagine, Dad: Nelly
the circus elephant down here bathing,
echt spouting floozy in the Jacuzzi

whiskied out and drunk above the cutbank.
High-plain hawk flew me out of the valley,
snow into mists, conjuring the Liffey.

Birds lifted in waves from the soft shoulder,
the winter wedding dispersing, Redl,
d'Annunzio, Uskoks with grappling hooks,

the Kaiser and the Archduke, flowing west.
*Build it up with silver and gold, silver
and gold, silver and gold, build it up with*

silver and gold, my fair lady. Goodbye
Barbara, goodbye Diana. *Silver
and gold will be stolen away, stolen...*

Goodbye Ethel, goodbye black-and-white cats.
Suppose the man should fall asleep? Goodbye
young Wallace, goodbye. Goodbye Eastend Blues.

*Give him a pipe to smoke all night, smoke all
night, smoke all night. Give him a pipe to smoke
all night, my fair lady.*

Acknowledgements

Gratitude to The Canada Council for support during the writing of these poems.

Thanks a lot to the folk who administer the Wallace Stegner House in Eastend, Saskatchewan, where *Pacific, that* and *Prairie, this* were written.

Thanks to John Barton and *The Malahat Review* for publishing "Extraction," to Moira MacDougall and *Literary Review of Canada* for publishing "Visitant," and to Ursula Vaira and Leaf Press for publishing the chapbook *Ottawa*.

And a deep thank you to Stan Dragland who so carefully listened and guided this manuscript to its final form.

Notes

The book's first epigraph is from *The Taittiriya Upanishad* (translated by Eknath Eswaran); the second is from Laura Riding's *Selected Poems: in Five Sets.* The epigraphs to the *Ottawa* sections are from T.S. Eliot's *Four Quartets.* The quotations attributed to Ken Dryden are from a talk he gave during the Ottawa Writers Festival in 2010. The stage directions in *I Waited at Mallaig* are from Shakespeare's *The Tempest.* The town of Eastend, Saskatchewan was called Whitemud when Wallace Stegner lived there, and the quotations in *Prairie, this* are taken from Stegner's *Wolf Willow* and *The Sound of Mountain Water.*

Michael Kenyon was born in Sale, England, and has lived on Canada's west coast since 1967. Author of fifteen books of poetry and fiction, his *The Beautiful Children* won the 2010 ReLit Award for best novel. Other work has been shortlisted for the Commonwealth Writers Prize, SmithBooks/Books in Canada First Novel Award, Baxter Hathaway Prize (Cornell) in fiction, *The Malahat Review* Novella Prize, *Prism International*'s fiction contest (won twice), the Journey Prize, and the National and Western Magazine Awards. Kenyon has been employed as a seaman, a diver, and a taxidriver. Presently he works as a freelance editor and a therapist, and lives in Victoria and on Pender Island, BC.

CREDIT: HARRY NEUFELD